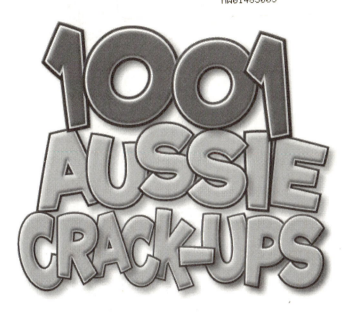

1001 AUSSIE CRACK-UPS

camp quality.

laughter is the best medicine.

camp quality.

laughter is the best medicine.

SCHOLASTIC
SYDNEY AUCKLAND NEW YORK TORONTO LONDON MEXICO CITY
NEW DELHI HONG KONG BUENOS AIRES PUERTO RICO

Scholastic Australia
ABN 11 000 614 577
PO Box 579
Gosford NSW 2250
www.scholastic.com.au

Part of the Scholastic Group
Sydney ● Auckland ● New York ● Toronto ● London ● Mexico City
● New Delhi ● Hong Kong ● Buenos Aires ● Puerto Rico

First published by Scholastic Australia as *501 Great Aussie Jokes* in 2008, and as *502
More Great Aussie Jokes in* 2009.
This edition published in 2012.
Text and illustrations copyright © Camp Quality 2008, 2009.
Special thanks to major contributors Jim Dewar and Sam Franzway.
Illustrations by Louis Shea.

National Library of Australia Cataloguing-in-Publication entry

Title:	1001 Aussie Crack-Ups / illustrated by Louis Shea.
ISBN:	9781742833194 (pbk.)
Target Audience:	For primary school age.
Subjects:	Australian wit and humour – Juvenile humour.
	Australia – Juvenile humour.
Other Authors/Contributors:	Shea, Louis.
Dewey Number:	A828.402

Typeset in Corky, Hank BT and House-A-Rama Kingpin.

Printed by Griffin Press.
Scholastic Australia's policy, in association with Griffin Press, is to use papers that are
renewable and made efficiently from wood grown in sustainable forests, so as to minimise
its environmental footprint.

FOREWORD

Did you know?

If you laugh 100 times a day it is the same amount of exercise as 15 minutes of rowing or jogging?

Here at Camp Quality we believe that laughter is the best medicine. So, to create a better life for every child living with cancer in Australia, we help them and their families to laugh by specialising in optimism, resilience and fun therapy! Fun therapy means that kids get the chance to forget about having cancer and get to have fun again. Their cancer takes a back seat so they can ride waves, ride horses, abseil down cliffs, paddle down rivers and slip down giant waterslides. A day, a weekend or a week in a fun, optimistic environment can make all the difference to a child's outlook and ability to deal with cancer.
This hilarious joke book was inspired in 2006 by Daniel Staunton, one of our CQ kids with an inoperable brain tumour. Six years on, Daniel is still bringing optimism and happiness to other CQ kids, with money from these joke books going towards funding our different programs.
Thanks for believing that laughter is the best medicine!

Simon Rountree
CEO Camp Quality

PS: Make Laughter the Best Medicine and tell us your favourite Aussie joke.
Visit campquality.org.au/yourjoke
or tweet#@camp_Quality

laughter is the best medicine.

Meet camp Quality

camp Quality is the children's family cancer charity that
believes in building optimism and resilience in the lives of children
and families affected by cancer through fun
therapy and education.

We believe that laughter is the best medicine.

At camp Quality, we are convinced that the caring for children
affected by cancer goes beyond medication and technology.
Our education, hospital, family support and recreational
programs play a crucial role in building a supportive, optimistic
community for our families nationwide.

You'll find that fun and optimism flows through all our
programs, our people and our culture. The fun we have is not
just for our families; everyone can share our culture. Visit our
website to see for yourself—

campquality.org.au

At CQ we love to share a joke. can you tell?

CONTENTS

BONZER BONANZA

What do Kangaroo,
Koala, Emu
and Wombat have
in common?

They have a birthday
every year!

What does Australia produce that
no other country produces?

Australians!

What's in the middle of Melbourne?

The letter O!

How do you get rid of a fly?

Tell it to buzz off!

Billy: How do you make a mattamate?

Mario: What's a mattamate?

Billy: Nothing, mate. What's a matter with you?

In which Australian city do the
most people with fuzzy hair live?

Frizz-bane!

Which Australian city likes
horse-riding the most?

Saddle-aide!

Which Australian city has the
cleanest people?

Ho-bath!

Which Australian town has the second
cleanest people?

Broome!

Which Australian city is the tastiest?

Canberry!

Which Australian city has the
most darts players?

Dartwin!

Which Australian city is full of jumping girls?

Alice Springs!

Which Australian town has everything on special?

Sale!

Which Australian town features a pleased boulder?

Gladstone!

Which Australian state has the biggest mammals?

New South Whales!

Why did the cockatoo sit on the alarm clock?

Because he wanted to be on time.

What's purple, sweet and stretches for 2600 kilometres off the coast of Queensland?

The Grape Barrier Reef!

One day Tom looked over his fence and saw his neighbour, Barry, throwing big handfuls of white powder all over his front lawn.

'What are you doing?' asked Tom.

'Well,' said Barry, 'I bought this powder from a man at the market. He said that if I spread it all over my lawn it would keep all the gorillas away!'

'But Barry,' said Tom, 'there aren't any gorillas around here!'

'I know,' answered Barry. 'Pretty good, isn't it?'

Why did the chicken cross the Royal Show?

To get to the other ride!

What did the farmer exclaim when his entry won 'best sheep' award at the show?

'Ewe beauty!'

Why did the Melbourne jockey enrol
in a tea-making course?

He hoped to make a good showing in the Cup.

What did the sentimental Aussie sing at the
barbecue?

A couple of old thongs.

Which classic Oz movie is set under
a Hills hoist?

'Picnic at Hanging Frock.'

Why does an Aussie avoid wearing
a big flappy shirt at a barbecue?

It snags on the barbie.

A Queenslander, a Victorian and a Western Australian are all sightseeing at the Sydney Centrepoint Tower. When they get up to the observation deck they notice a sign: 'Win $1 million!' and a tour guide standing next to it.

'What's the story?' they ask the guide.

'Well, it's a Centrepoint challenge. If you can take your watch off, drop it over the balcony and run down all the stairs in time to catch it, you win the million dollars!'

'Crikey!' says the Queenslander. 'I'll give that a go!' So he takes his watch off, drops it over the edge and charges down the stairs. 250 metres below he rushes out onto the street, only to find his watch shattered on the footpath.

'No problem,' says the Victorian. 'Too many bananas, not enough speed.' He throws his watch over the side and sprints down the stairs as fast as he can go. But, when he bursts onto the street, he is also too late to catch his watch.

The Western Australian just smiles. 'This million bucks is as good as mine.' He unstraps his watch, tosses it over the edge and strolls towards the stairs. He walks down onto Pitt

Street, makes his way over to the Opera House, takes some photos, picks up a few souvenirs for the folks back home, does a bit of shopping, has a coffee, walks back to Centrepoint Tower and catches his watch.

'How did you do that?' cries the guide, writing him the million-dollar cheque.

'Easy,' he replies. 'I'm from Western Australia, mate. My watch is two hours slow!'

In which Aussie city do the residents slip and slide?

Skidney.

Why did the cat cross the road?

Because it purr furs the other side.

Why can't an emu fly?

It never books a flight.

Did you hear about the optimistic kangaroo?

It hopped for the best.

Which classic Oz movie features
a tin and lots of wild horses?

The Can from Snowy River.

Which bird is mixed up with two gangs?

The gang-gang cockatoo.

What do you call a boomerang
that won't come back?

A stick.

Why did the netballer join a rifle club?

She wanted to improve her shooting.

Which classic Oz movie involves a parrot that goes to New York and has a huge knife?

Cockatoo Dundee.

Which Aussie capital city is for men only?

Manberra.

Which Aussie town is just piles of stones?

Cairns.

Which Aussie town is a little wetter than most?

Dampier.

Which Aussie town is too hot to touch?

Burnie.

In which Aussie city does Homer Simpson
fling his son around?

Throwbart.

In which Aussie city do smart businesspeople live?

Bizbrain.

In which Aussie city do ships tie up?

Berth.

Which Aussie town has a population of winged
creatures as residents?

Birdsville.

In which Aussie state do the most crazy people live?

Tasmaniac.

Which Aussie town has heaps and heaps
of Indian food?

Tuncurry.

Who would open the batting for the Aussie animal cricket team?

Wombat and numbat.

Which region of Australia is feared by people who have to lift heavy weights?

The out-back.

Where do Aussie mozzies get buried?

A mozzie-leum.

Why did the lorikeet join the army?

It wanted to be a parrot-trooper.

Why did the girl put dust under
her pillow?

She wanted sweep dreams.

Where did the gum tree go for its holiday?

To the beech.

How did it prepare for its holiday?

It packed its trunk.

Did it find its way there OK?

Yes, its trip was well plant.

How long did it take to get there?

Tree hours.

How do you know that for sure?

It kept a log.

Did the local newspaper do a story on the gum tree's departure?

Yes. The headline read: 'Gum Leaves'.

Would it do it all again?

It wood.

What's the name for river bottoms in Australia?

Down under down under.

Why does the kookaburra laugh?

It thinks everyone else is a galah.

Which shy Aussie animal is spotted every day?

The spotted quoll.

What's Australia's longest river, sweetheart?

The Murray, Darling.

Which Australian umpire can be seen
from space?

The Great Barrier Ref.

Which aircraft do outback kangaroos prefer?

The Nullarbor Plane.

Which Australian bird can't help
telling fibs?

The lyrebird.

What did the Australian flag say to the pole?

Nothing, it just waved.

Why did the wallaby cross the road?

Because it was the chicken's day off.

Lote Tuqiri—sports personality.

CELEBRITY CRACK-UPS!

Outback hotel clerk: How did you sleep?

Guest: Like a baby.

Outback hotel clerk: You woke up crying every two hours with a wet nappy?

What's red and hangs in a eucalyptus tree?

A stupid strawberry.

What do you get when you cross a cockatoo with a homing pigeon?

A bird that is not afraid to ask for directions.

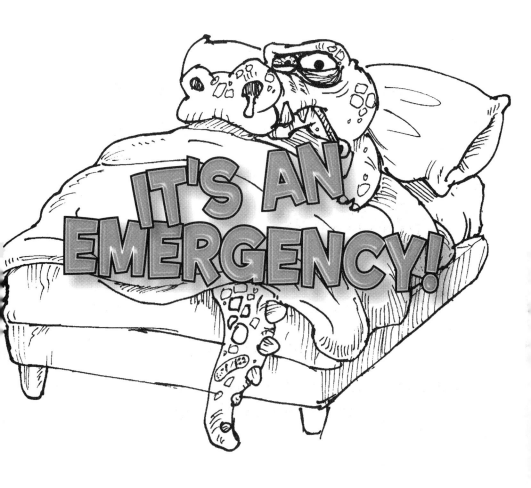

Which Australian reptile is always sick?

A crookodile.

Why did the doctor become depressed when examining the patient's foot?

He felt a heel.

Caller: 'Doctor! Come quickly!
My daughter has swallowed my car keys!'

Doctor: 'Don't panic. I'm on my way.
What have you done in the meantime?'

Caller: 'Oh, I'm using my husband's car.'

Patient: 'Doctor, will I be able to play the piano
after the operation?'

Doctor: 'Of course you will.'

Patient: 'That's amazing! Up til now I couldn't . . .'

Patient: 'I am a wigwam,
I am a teepee. I am a wigwam, I am a teepee.'

Doctor: 'Ahh, your problem is you are two tents.'
(too tense)

Patient: 'Doctor! I keep thinking I am a dustbin.'

Doctor: 'Rubbish!'

Patient: 'Doctor, I feel like a pack of cards!'

Doctor: 'I'll deal with you later!'

Doctor: 'I'll be with you shortly,
Mr Godzilla. Have a seat while
you're waiting.'

Mr Godzilla: 'No thanks, I'm not hungry.'

Patient: 'Doctor, doctor, I can't sleep!'

Doctor: 'Lie on the edge of your
bed and you'll soon drop off!'

Patient: 'Doctor doctor, I got stuck
in a freezer!'

Doctor: 'Are you OK?'

Patient: 'Yeah, I'm cool.'

An Aussie woman brought a very limp dingo in to a veterinary surgery. As she laid her pet on the table, the vet pulled out his stethoscope and listened to the dingo's chest. After a moment or two, the vet shook his head sadly and said, 'I'm so sorry, your dingo "Cuddles" has passed away.'

The distressed owner wailed, 'Are you sure?'

'Yes, I am sure. The dingo is dead,' he replied.

'How can you be so sure?' she protested, 'I mean, you haven't done any testing on him or anything. He might just be in a coma!' The vet rolled his eyes, turned around and left the room, returning a few moments later with a black Labrador Retriever. As the dingo's owner looked on in amazement, the dog stood on his hind legs, put his front paws on the examination table and sniffed the dingo from top to bottom. He then looked at the vet with sad eyes and shook his head. The vet patted the dog and took it out, and returned a few moments later with a cat. The cat jumped up on the table and also sniffed delicately at the dingo from head to foot. The cat sat back on its haunches, shook its head, meowed softly and strolled out of the room.

The vet looked at the woman and said, 'I'm sorry, but as I've already told you, this is most definitely, 100% certifiably, a dead dingo.' Then the vet turned to his computer terminal, hit a few keys and produced a bill, which he handed to the woman. The dingo's owner, still in shock, took the bill.

'$400!' she cried. '$400 . . . just to tell me my dingo is dead?!'

The vet shrugged. 'I'm sorry, but if you'd taken my word for it in the first place, the bill would have been $60. But with the Lab Report and the Cat Scan, it's now gone up to $400.'

Patient: 'Doctor, I'm worried about these terrible blemishes on my skin.'

Doctor: 'Take this cream and use it every night for a month.'

Patient: 'Are you sure it'll work?'

Doctor: 'I never make rash promises.'

Caller: 'Doctor! I've swallowed my son's iPod!'

Doctor: 'You must be choking!'

Caller: 'No, I'm serious!'

Patient: 'Doctor, doctor I feel like I'm invisible.'

Doctor: 'Next please.'

Why did the rabbit go to the hospital?

Because it needed an hoperation.

Patient: 'Doctor, I think I'm a kangaroo, surrounded by kangaroos.'

Doctor: 'Stop bouncing and we'll go to my pouch to talk about it.'

Why did the banana go to the doctor?

Because it wasn't peeling well.

What do you call a doll with a headache?

Pana-doll.

Patient: 'I feel very weak and I'm extremely hungry.'

Doctor: 'Hmm, I see you have a lamington in your ear and a sausage up your nose. Clearly you're not eating properly.'

Caller: 'Doctor! We're stuck in traffic on the way to hospital and my wife is about to have a baby!'

Doctor: 'Is this her first child?'

Caller: 'Don't be ridiculous! This is her husband!'

An Aussie bloke goes into the doctor's office and says that his body hurts wherever he touches it. 'Impossible!' says the doctor. 'Show me.' The bloke takes his finger, presses on his left shoulder and screams. Then he pushes on his elbow and screams even more. He pushes his knee and screams. Likewise, he pushes his ankle and screams. Everywhere he touches makes him scream. 'I think I know the problem,' the doctor says. 'Your finger is broken.'

Doctor: 'I've got bad news and good news.'

Patient: 'What's the bad news?'

Doctor: 'You've got a serious heart condition.'

Patient: 'What's the good news?'

Doctor: 'I've just won the lottery.'

What do you give a dog with a fever?

Mustard. (It's good for a hot dog.)

An Aussie bloke walked into the doctor's surgery with a problem. The bloke said, 'Doctor! I have a serious problem, I can never remember what I just said.'

'When did you first notice this problem?' the doctor enquired.

'What problem?'

Kate Ritchie—TV and radio personality

CELEBRITY CRACK-UPS!

Why don't pirates have headache pills?

Because the parrots-eat-'em-all. (paracetamol)

Why did the farmer take his cow to the psychiatrist?

Because she was moooody.

Why was the chicken sick?

Because he had peoplepox!

Which tree has a sore mouth?

Red gum.

What animal goes 'Aaa'?

A sheep with a blocked nose.

What kind of sickness do dinosaurs get?

Bronto-sore-us!

GOOD TUCKER

Which bird can make you breakfast,
lunch and dinner?

A cook-aburra!

Which vegetable loves athletics?

The runner bean.

How is a chicken like a grape?

They both have feathers, except for the grape.

Which vegetable is always a bit damp?

Leek.

Why is it a waste of time trying to find
a missing lettuce?

It's a lost cos.

Which vegetable has been in a fight?

Black-eyed pea!

What are two things a penguin cannot
eat for dinner?

Breakfast and lunch.

What do you call
a nervous carrot?

An edgy-vegie!

Store owner: 'Good morning Janet! What can I get for you?'

Janet: 'Something for dinner, please.'

Store owner: 'I have some lovely fresh ox tongue!'

Janet: 'Oh, no! Yuck! I couldn't eat something that comes out of an animal's mouth! I'll just have a dozen eggs.'

Which fruit went to sea?

Navel orange.

Judge: 'Order in the court!'

Convict: 'I'll have a hamburger and fries!'

How does a sugary liquid stop you lounging at your desk?

It makes you syrup straight.

A guy sits alone in a hotel lounge one night enjoying a quiet drink when he suddenly hears a voice . . .

'Nice shirt.'

He looks around but there's no-one else in the room except for the waiter way up the other end. He puts the voice down to a long week in the office and goes back to his drink. A minute later he hears the voice again . . .

'Nice tie, goes well with the suit. Is it Italian?'

The guy spins around, looks up and down the place but again, there's no one to be seen but the waiter, polishing glasses down the far end. He turns back to his drink.

'I like your haircut, pal. Very sharp.'

The guy is starting to worry for his sanity and calls to the waiter, 'Excuse me mate, are you talking to me?'

'No,' replies the waiter. 'Why?'

'I just keep hearing this voice saying nice things to me,' says the guy.

'Oh, that'd be the peanuts,' says the waiter. 'They're complimentary.'

Ben Lawson, Actor

Why does the baked potato leave its
mobile phone on?

In case the onion rings.

Which fruit goes around in twos?

Pears!

In the old days, what did you
call fast food?

Food you couldn't catch!

Which fruit keeps hedges neat?

Prune.

What's the yummiest day of the week?

Sundae.

What's big and white?

A fridge.

Did you hear about the poor bloke who
arranged for a home-delivered pizza and then
forgot where he'd ordered it?

He didn't know where his
next meal was coming from.

Which fruit has two feet?

Pawpaw!

Which fruit do you find in a calendar?

Date!

Which fruit is always breaking down?

Lemon!

What's sweet, yellow and extremely dangerous?

Shark-infested custard.

Did you hear about the wealthy baker?

He had two Rolls!

Which herb is just silly?

Dill!

Why do the French eat snails?

Because they like slow food!

What did one plate say to the other?

Lunch is on me!

How do you keep a hungry lion
from charging?

Take away its credit card.

What do you get when you cross a
baguette with Swiss cheese?

Hole-meal bread.

What do you call a bunch of barbies
standing in a row?

A barbie queue.

*Matt Moran—Aria restaurant,
celebrity chef on Masterchef and
The Chopping Block*

What do termites eat for breakfast?

Oakmeal.

Where do parents keep the baby food?

In the mushroom.

A lady went into a butcher shop complaining about the sausages she had just bought. 'The middle is meat,' she exclaimed, 'but the ends are sawdust!'

'Well,' said the butcher, 'these days it's hard to make ends meat.'

A bloke goes to a bakery that specialises in crazy-shaped bread. There are loaves shaped like kangaroos and cars and hats. He buys one that looks like a chessboard and takes it home. But when he goes to make a sandwich he finds that his new loaf of bread is as hard as a rock, so he takes it back to the bakery.

When the baker asks why he's bringing it back, he replies, 'It's stale mate.'

The baker doesn't believe him and refuses to return his money. So the bloke shows the loaf to the baker and says, 'Check mate!'

Where do baby cows eat?

The calf-eteria.

What's the difference between brussels sprouts and snot?

No kid will eat brussels sprouts!

What do you always eat with your eyes open?

See food!

How do code-breakers like their eggs
in the morning?

Scrambled.

Why didn't the hot dog act in the play?

The roll wasn't good enough.

What do pandas eat for breakfast?

Pandacakes!

What happens to a ladyfinger banana
when you leave it out in the rain?

It gets wet.

Is it usual to see an underdone steak at an Aussie barbie?

No, it's quite rare.

Billy: 'What's the special today?'

Waiter: 'It's bean soup.'

Billy: 'Yes, but what is it now?'

Which country wants the most food?

Hungary!

Why are tomatoes round and red?

Because if they were long and yellow,
they'd be bananas!

What's grumpy and goes really well
with ice-cream?

Apple grumble.

What did the pun say to the egg?

Is this a yolk?

Mum: 'Sandy! Eat your spinach!
It's good for growing children!'

Sandy: 'But I don't want to grow any children!'

What's a sheep's favourite thing to eat?

A baaaanana.

Which big animal makes a yummy dessert?

A jellyphant.

What did the rabbit say to the carrot?

It's been nice gnawing you!

What do you get when you ask a lemon
for help?

Lemon-aid.

Why was it that only tall people were invited
to the barbecue?

Because the steaks were so high.

Why did the security guards attend the barbecue?

In case there was a flare-up.

What does a barbecue defend itself with?

A karate chop.

Two peanuts ran into a tunnel, but only one reappeared. What happened to the other one?

He was assaulted! (a salted)

What's the term for soldiers who sneak away from their posts to eat pudding?

Desserters.

Why does everyone love Mr Mushroom?

Because he's a fungi! (fun guy)

Why were the little strawberries upset?

Because their parents were in a jam!

How does the clairvoyant like her steak?

Medium.

'Mum, have you cooked dinner yet?'

'I've cooked the chicken soup.'

'How about something for me too?!'

Why was the tomato sauce embarrassed?

It saw the salad dressing.

Why are red lollies so popular?

'Cos they're such sweeties.

'Mum, what are we having for dinner tonight?'

'Y.M.C.A.'

'What?'

'Yesterday's Meal Cooked Again.'

Where was a much-loved dessert
wiped out?

At Custard's Last Stand.

What pop stars are lots of lollies
really into?

Wrappers.

One day there were three tomatoes walking down the street—a mama tomato, a daddy tomato and a baby tomato. The baby tomato was walking too slowly, so daddy tomato went back, stepped on him and said, 'KETCHUP!'

Sara Groen—presenter for Seven News, It Takes Two

Diner (studying the menu): 'The venison seems extremely expensive!'

Waiter: 'That's because it's deer, madam.'

Diner: 'My soup bowl is leaking.'

Waiter: 'That's because you're having leek soup, sir.'

Diner: 'This fish is off!'

Waiter: 'Golly! A travelling fish!
Where is it off to?'

Diner: 'Young man, I'll have coffee,
with no cream.'

Waiter: 'I'm afraid we're right out
of cream, madam . . .
will you take it without milk instead?'

Diner: 'Waiter! Why is my bowl full of pieces of
coral? I ordered beef soup!'

Waiter: 'Sorry, sir. I thought you said
"reef" soup.'

Waiter: 'Would you like your steak rare, sir?'

Diner: 'Well done.'

Waiter: 'Thank you, sir. Rare it is, then.'

Diner: 'Waiter, why is there a dog in my soup bowl?
I asked for noodle soup!'

Waiter: 'Sorry, madam. I thought you
ordered poodle soup.'

Diner: 'Waiter, there's a fly in my soup!'

Waiter: 'Who's there?'

Diner: 'Eh?'

Waiter: 'Oops! Sorry, madam
—I'm in the wrong joke!'

Why did the jelly baby go to school?

It wanted to be a smartie.

Why didn't the waiters place the desserts on
the left side of the table settings?

They were concentrating on pudding things right.

What sweet is just too big to eat?

A dining-room sweet.

What do you call cheese that doesn't belong to you?

Nacho cheese!

Why did the boy throw butter out the window?

He wanted to see a butterfly.

How did the nut sneeze?

He said 'cashew'.

HISTORICAL HOWLERS

What flag did junior pirates fly?

The school and crossbones.

How did serfs who lived near the sea amuse themselves?

They took part in their local serf lifesaving championships.

Did you hear about the pirate captain
who loved pudding?

He sailed the seven seas looking
for dessert islands.

Did you hear about the pirate queen
who wanted more hairs on her eyelids?

She was given 100 lashes.

Did you hear about the underperforming arrow?

It got shot.

Did you hear about the underperforming cannonball?

It got fired.

What did the Vikings use to send secret messages?

Norse code.

Who was sobbing in the village square?

The town crier.

Why did the pirate ship's resident minstrel
go ashore on the desert island?

He was looking for somewhere to bury his lute.

Did you hear about the ship's mast that wasn't there?

It was a mizzen.

Did you hear about the rebellious peasants who
hadn't washed for weeks?

They were revolting.

Did you hear about the obstinate pirate
who got covered in glue?

He stuck to his guns.

Which ancient world celebrity
invented room service?

Helen of Tray.

Mahatma Gandhi, as you know, walked barefoot most of the time, which produced an impressive set of calluses on his feet. He also ate very little, which made him rather frail and with his odd diet, he suffered from bad breath. This made him (oh man this is so bad it's good) . . . a super-calloused-fragile-mystic-hexed-by-halitosis!

Stephen Michael King—children's author and illustrator

CELEBRITY CRACK-UPS!

Did you hear about the poet who wasn't allowed into the castle?

He was bard.

Why was the king's army so tired?

It had a lot of sleepless knights.

What men of religion were best at holding
medieval barbecues?

Friars.

What terrible disease swept through
the fireplaces of the medieval world?

The grate plague.

Why did the minstrel look puzzled?

He was a wondering minstrel.

Which country had the most pirates?

Arrr-gentina!

Which ancient city never stays still?

Roam.

Why did the pirate captain suddenly
want to go shopping?

He spotted a sale on the horizon.

Why did the pirate look in the dictionary?

To see how to spell 'R'!

Why do Komodo dragons sleep all day?

So that they can stay up
and fight knights!

How do you make a pheromone?

- (Pharaoh-moan.)

Knock over his pyramid.

WALL.E—Disney PIXAR

**CELEBRITY
CRACK-UPS!**

WILDLIFE WOWZERS

Why do mother kangaroos hate bad weather?

Because the joeys have to play inside!

Why did the crocodile cross the road?

It was following the chicken . . .

Why did the crocodile cross the road again?

He was a double-crosser!

Why did the emu cross the road?

To prove he wasn't a chicken.

How do you get info on spiders?

Easy. There are hundreds of websites available.

What's a green tree frog's favourite drink?

Croak-a-Cola!

Why did the stockman ride his horse?

Because it was too heavy to carry!

What do you get when you cross a glove with a
Tasmanian Devil?

I don't know, but I wouldn't shake hands with it!

What time is it when there are
twelve hungry dingoes at your front door?

Time to leave by the back door.

What do you call a sheep that dances?

A Baallerina.

Why did the goanna climb over
the glass wall?

To see what was on the other side!

What do you call a platypus trapped
under a rock?

A flatypus!

Why did the Aussie seabird believe everything it heard?

It was soooo gullible.

Did you hear about the cagebird that simply would not move?

It refused to budgie.

What do rosellas use for napkins?

Flapkins!

How do you catch a unique kookaburra?

U-nique up on him!

How do you catch a tame kookaburra?

Tame way.

What's cute, cuddly and bright purple?

A koala holding his breath!

What sound do echidnas make when they kiss?

Ouch!

What do you get when you cross
a kangaroo with a sheep?

A woolly jumper!

What do you get when you cross a frog
and a crocodile?

A croakadile.

Who delivers presents to young
Great White Sharks at Christmas?

Santa Jaws!

Why did Wally Wombat pour a glass of
water onto the ground?

He wanted to make a splash!

What is kangaroo skin mostly used for?

To hold kangaroos together.

Which animal can jump higher
than Mount Everest?

a) Wally Wombat

b) Katey Kangaroo

c) Eddie Emu

d) Any of the above, because
mountains can't jump!

What do you call a dingo that's disappeared?

A dingone.

Why did the koala fall out of the tree?

He was asleep.

Why did the second koala fall out of the tree?

He was stapled to the first koala.

Why did the third koala fall out
of the tree?

Peer pressure.

Why did the fourth koala fall out of the tree?

He thought it was a game.

Why did the fifth koala fall out of the tree?

He was hit by a fridge!

What happens when a kangaroo
and a giraffe cross paths?

Broken legs!

What type of umbrella would
an emu have on a rainy day?

A wet one!

What did the echidna say to the cactus?

Are you my mother?

Where do sheep go to get a haircut?

The baa-baa's.

What do you get when you cross
a cat with a platypus?

A platypuss.

Why did the freezing seagull fly onto
the telephone line?

It wanted to chatter!

What do Aussie cats like to climb?

The Blue Meowntins.

MUSICAL MADNESS

What pet animal sits in its cage
making melodic noises?

A humster.

What's a chicken's favourite instrument?

Cluckstanets.

What do you get when you
drop a piano down a mineshaft?

A flat minor.

What do you get when you
drop a piano on an army camp?

A flat major.

What instrument do elephants play?

The trumpet!

How do you make a bandstand?

Hide all their chairs!

Why do some rock'n'roll bands wreck
the platforms they play on?

It's just a stage they go through!

What is it called when a person sings in the shower?

A soap opera.

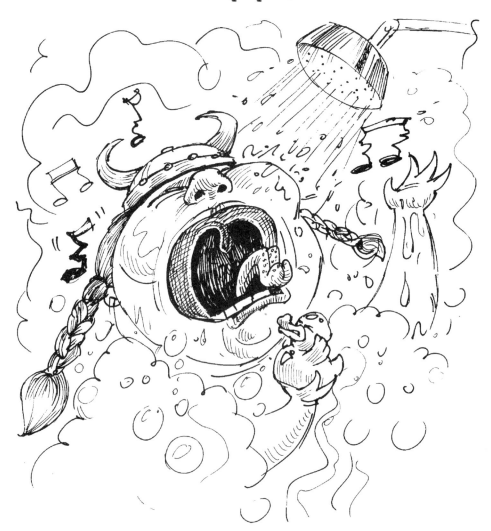

What kind of music does that new group,
The Grandfathers, play?

Pop music.

What kind of music does that new group,
The Parcels, play?

Wrap.

What kind of music does that new group,
Jumping Pelvis, play?

Hip-hop.

What kind of music does that new group,
The Jumbucks, play?

Baa-rock!

What kind of music does that new group,
The Zoo Animals, play?

Cage-in.

What kind of music does that new group,
Playground Equipment, play?

Swing!

What kind of music does that new group,
Sapphire Navy, play?

Blues!

Who is the bee's favourite singer?

Sting!

Which famous composer could never be found?

Haydn.

What is a sailor's favourite musical note?

A sea flat.

Why did the rock go to the disco?

'Cos it wanted to rock'n'roll.

Which famous composer always leaned to one side?

Liszt!

How is a banana skin like music?

Because if you don't C sharp you will B flat.

Why did the Aussie bass player travel to the foothills of the Himalayas?

He heard there was a bass camp there.

Who is the bee's favourite pop group?

The Bee Gees!

Why was the orchestra's
documentary movie banned?

It featured scenes of
shocking violins.

What do players in the orchestra's
brass section use to clean their teeth?

A tuba toothpaste.

What instrument do rodents
like to play?

The mouse organ.

What instrument do people play
in marshy parts of Scotland?

The bogpipes.

What instrument do Scottish insects play?

The bugpipes.

A ZOO-NIVERSE OF CRITTERS

What do you call a bear with no ears?

A 'b'!

Where are foals born?

Horsepital.

What goes black, white, black, white, black, white?

A zebra stuck in a revolving door.

How do you fit four elephants into a Mini?

Two in the front, two in the back.

How do you fit four giraffes into a Mini?

There's no room. It's full of elephants.

How can you tell if there's an elephant
in your refrigerator?

The milk smells like peanuts.

How can you tell if there are two elephants
in your refrigerator?

They always giggle when the light goes out.

How can you tell if there are
three elephants
in your refrigerator?

You can't close the door.

How can you tell if there are
four elephants
in your refrigerator?

There's a Mini parked outside.

How can you fit a dinosaur into
a Mini?

It doesn't matter, the elephants
were there first!

How do you get down off a duck?

What were you doing up there
in the first place?

There are two monkeys in a bath.
One says 'Ooo, ooo, ooo!'
The other says,
'If it's too hot, put some cold in!'

Pip Russell—television presenter

Why didn't the dinosaur cross the road?

Because roads weren't invented.

What do you use to get antlers to grow out of your hair?

Moose.

Did you hear about the dog that lost its temper?

It hit the woof.

What kind of monkey can fly?

A hot-air baboon.

What do you call a collection of primates?

A barrel of monkeys!

What do you call a field of giggling cows?

Laughing stock.

Why couldn't the bee contact his
friend on the phone?

He kept getting a buzzy signal.

What do you get when your dog
has its sixth birthday?

A six-year-old dog.

How do you know if you're in bed with an elephant?

The pillow smells like peanuts.

What do you call a sleeping bull?

A bulldozer.

What goes cluck, cluck, cluck, BOOM?

A chicken in a minefield!

What do hippopotamuses have that
nothing else has?

Baby hippopotamuses.

What do you get when you cross
a chicken with an elephant?

Really big eggs!

What do you get when you mix a
Tyrannosaurus with explosives?

Dino-mite!

What's the difference between the sky
and a lion with a thorn in its paw?

One pours with rain
and the other roars with pain!

Where do baby apes sleep?

In ape-ri-cots.

Where do you find a dog with no legs?

Right where you left him!

A duck goes into a store and waddles up to the manager. He asks him if he sells duck food. The manager tells him no. The duck leaves.

The next day the duck returns and asks again. The manager still does not sell duck food. The duck leaves.

The next day, the duck returns again. He asks the same question. The manager says no and warns the duck if he asks one more time he will staple the duck's feet to the floor.

For the fourth time, the duck goes back into the store. He asks, 'Do you have any staples?' The manager tells him no.

Then the duck says, 'Do you have any duck food?'

Why do elephants never forget?

What do they have to remember?

Why are intelligent ducks like comedians?

They're always making wisequacks.

How do apes protect themselves against invaders?

They organise gorilla campaigns.

Why do old snakes complain?

Fangs aren't what they used to be.

Why are elephant herds in such demand at employment agencies?

They are really good at multi-tusking.

What did the disapproving mother
elephant say to her little one?

Tusk, tusk!

What kind of printer does a pig use?

An oinkjet!

What did one elephant say to the other elephant?

Have you seen my tail?

Why was the duckling trying to make
its mum laugh?

Because she was feeling down.

Did you hear about the sad duckling who tucked his head into his feathers?

He felt down.

Which dog is always ready for a fight?

A boxer.

How does a poodle say hello in France?

Bone-jour!

What do you call adventurous budgies?

Trillseekers.

How did the mare know she was going to have a foal?

She felt a little horse.

What do you call a group of rabbits hopping backwards?

A receding hareline!

Steve Jacobs—Weather Presenter, Today

Why did the headline 'Lame Wildebeest!' appear on the front page of the newspaper?

It was a slow gnus day.

Why did Mrs Fly fly?

Because Mr Spider spied'er.

What did the young spider want
to be when she grew up?

A web designer.

What do you call a singing antelope?

A chantelope.

Which big animal likes to watch TV?

A tellyphant.

What animal should you never play cards with?

A cheetah.

Why did the dog sit under the tree?

Because he didn't want to be a hot dog.

Why did the lion cross the road?

To get to the mane event.

How do dinosaurs smell?

With their noses!

**What sort of noise kept prehistoric
people awake at night?**

Dino-snores!

What did one firefly say to the other firefly?

'I don't like it here. Let's glow somewhere else.'

Why do elephants have all those wrinkles?

Because they don't fit on an ironing board!

How did the dog stop the DVD player?

He used the PAWS button.

There were ten cats in a boat. One jumped out.
How many were left?

None, they were all copycats.

What did the mosquito say to his friend?

'Do you want to go get a bite?'

What did one bee say to the other bee?

'Want some honey, Honey?'

What did the bee say when he got to the hive?

'Honey, I'm home!'

Why did the chicken cross the road?

Because the duck threw it.

Why did it cross back over again?

To go get the duck.

Where do frogs keep their money?

In riverbanks!

What kind of birds live in tin trees?

Toucans!

What was the heading of the
newspaper ad for the baby insect?

'Flea to a good home.'

Why did the chicken cross the road, roll in the mud,
and cross the road again?

Because it was a dirty double-crosser.

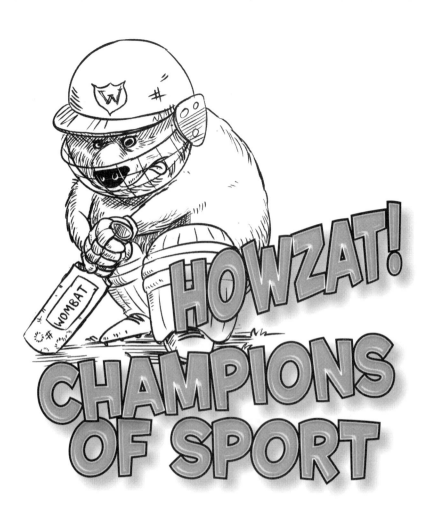

HOWZAT! CHAMPIONS OF SPORT

How do Aussie cricketers stay cool?

They sit next to their fans.

What goes all around a cricket oval but never moves?

The boundary line.

Why was the Aussie athlete so easy
to get along with?

Because he was always willing to discus things!

Did you hear about the Aussie champion
who broke her ankle while tap dancing?

She fell into the sink.

When is a baby good at basketball?

When it dribbles!

Matt Suleau—Reporter, Channel Ten

CELEBRITY CRACK-UPS!

Why are goalkeepers always the wealthiest?

They really know how to save.

Which footy code do you play without boots?

Socker.

Why couldn't the team of gum-tree sketch artists win a cricket match?

They always drew!

Why is Cinderella the worst sportsperson
in the world?

Because she has a pumpkin for a coach.

What's the difference between a cricketer
and a dog?

The cricketer has a complete uniform,
but the dog only pants!

What sport do photographers play?

Clickit.

When do Aussie golfers drive off?

Tee time.

Did you hear about the Aussie golfer who
forced a canary to play a shot for him?

He made a birdie putt.

Why did the golfer take two pairs of pants to the game?

In case he got a hole in one!

Kerri-Anne Kennerley—television personality and entertainer

CELEBRITY CRACK-UPS!

Why was the footballer angry with

the dressmaker?

She sold him a dummy.

Which world-famous footballer can fly like a bird?

Pele can.

How do you join a footy team?

Glue the players together.

What flavour chips does the
Australian gymnastics team eat?

Somersalt and vinegar!

Why did the Aussie golfer have to walk home?

He couldn't find his driver.

Why was the sprinter under pressure in her
qualifying race?

The heat was on.

Why was the cricketer unhappy
with his part in the horror movie?

He played a dead bat.

Why didn't the linesman take his job seriously?

It was just a sideline.

Did you hear about the messy soccer player?

He dribbled a lot.

Did you hear about the hopeless
midfielder who died?

His passing was regrettable.

Did you hear about the champion athlete
who gave up the discus, shot-put and javelin?

He threw it all away.

Why was the soccer player happy to be fouled?

She got a kick out of it.

Why did the speedy soccer player get into trouble
with the groundsman?

He was always tearing up the field.

Why did the high-scoring batsman rush
to the toilet?

He had the runs.

Why was the batsman accused of theft?

He nicked the ball.

How did the batsman rip his trousers?

He got caught on the fence.

How do you know the batsman
isn't at home?

The umpire says he's out.

Did you hear about the boring batsman?

He needed to get out more.

Why did the bowler fall asleep?

He was over-tired.

Why couldn't the batsman explain how he got out?

He was stumped.

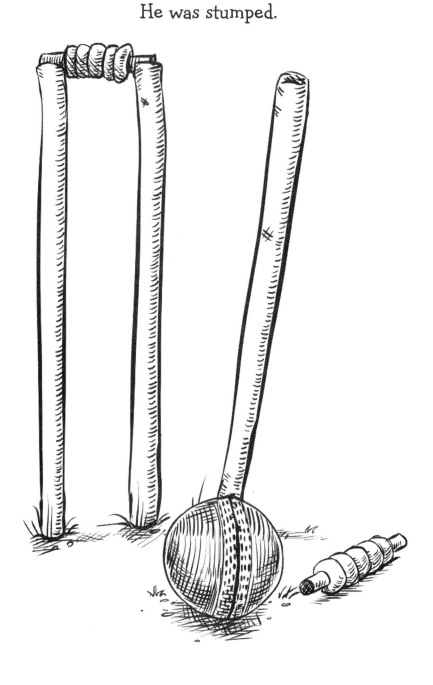

Why are Australian Open tennis umpires really smart people?

They know the score.

Why wasn't the marathoner worried?

She knew everything would be OK in the long run.

Why did the ball girl fetch a drink for the umpire?

She thought he had called for juice.

How did the Socceroos feel when their ball burst?

Deflated.

Why was the tennis equipment manufacturer so noisy?

He was always making a racquet.

Why did the tennis player have only herself
to blame for serving badly?

It was her own fault.

Why did the waiter make a good tennis player?

He was an excellent server.

Was that tennis movie, 'The Winning Shot',
a success at the box office?

Yes, it was a smash.

Why was the tennis racquet so nervous?

It was very highly strung.

Why didn't the tennis veteran need a lighter?

He had lots of matches under his belt.

Why did the pole vaulter get blamed
for everything?

It was always his vault.

Bluey: 'Are those your running shoes?'

Bazza: 'No, they're Spike's.'

Why did the veteran runner have trouble leaving his front yard?

He had a very stiff gait.

Why did the tennis player carry an extra set of wristbands?

In case he lost the first set.

Why did the tennis player carry a third set of wristbands?

In case he lost the first two sets.

Where do ghosts play tennis?

On a tennis corpse!

Lleyton Hewitt, tennis champion

CELEBRITY CRACK-UPS!

Why did the runner carry her dog's leash
in her races?

So she could tell her friends she took the lead.

Why was the dairy farmer such a good sprinter?

He had big calves.

Why was the successful striker completely satisfied?

She had achieved all her goals.

What happened to the soccer player
with a postage stamp on her head?

She got sent off.

Why must all batsmen be good swimmers?

In case they get caught in the deep.

Why did the soccer player have rolls
of turf in her car?

She ran onto the playing field and
took a corner.

What has four wheels and flies?

A garbage truck.

HUMDINGER LAUGHS

Did you hear about the little boy who was named after his father?

They called him Dad.

Janet: 'My little girl Suzy is only two, but she's been walking since she was nine months old!'

Tracey: 'She must be very tired . . .'

What's brown and sticky?

A stick.

Shelley Craft—Host, Australia's Funniest Home Videos

CELEBRITY CRACK-UPS!

Little Sally: 'Dad! Can I have another glass of water?'

Dad: 'But I've given you nine glasses already! Are you really that thirsty?'

Little Sally: 'No! My bedroom's still on fire!'

Why did Billy put spectacles on his dad's timber saw?

He wanted a see-saw!

What is a baby's motto?

If at first you don't succeed, cry and cry again!

If a red house is made out of red bricks and a blue house is made out of blue bricks, what is a green house made out of?

Glass!

Which months have 28 days?

All of them!

What do you call a bloke with a shovel on his head?

Doug.

What do you call a bloke hiding in a paper bag?

Russell.

Why do you always find things
in the last place you look?

Because after you find it, you stop looking!

What do you call a bloke with a seagull on his head?

Cliff.

Why was the full stop set free?

It had finished its sentence.

What kind of clothes do
aquariums wear?

Tank tops!

What are the last things
Australians take off before
going to bed?

Their feet off the floor!

Can a book change colour?

Yes. If it's not red when you begin reading it,
it'll be red when you've finished.

Why did the computer novice
buy tiny curtains for his screen?

He'd just installed windows.

Where do you go to weigh a pie?

Somewhere, over the rainbow,
weigh a pie!

Which plant is useful for washing the dishes?

Bottlebrush!

A man walks into a bar . . . Ouch!

*Adam Elliot — Animation Director,
Harvie Krumpet, Mary and Max*

Which plant loves to be part of a blizzard?

Snowdrop.

Which tree looks neat and tidy?

Spruce.

Which tree is well-liked by all the other trees?

Poplar!

Which tree is full of sand?

Beech.

Which tree has really bad handwriting?

Scribbly gum.

What do you call a woman sitting on a toothpick?

Olive.

What did the zero say to
the eight at the party?

Nice belt.

*Ed Phillips—radio and television
personality, reporter for The Circle*

**CELEBRITY
CRACK-UPS!**

**Did you hear about Darren, the hungry
16-year-old?**

He eight and eight.

Did you hear about Sheila, the hungry 32-year-old?

She eight and eight and eight and eight!

What did one paint tin say to the other?

'Can you cover for me?'

Why were the fern and the
palm happy to see each other?

They were old fronds.

What did the digital clock say to the
analog clock?

'Look ma, no hands!'

A couple attended a fancy dress party.
The bloke gave his girlfriend a piggy back
ride. Then he said at the door,
'We came here as a turtle.'

'So who is she?' asked the doorman.

The bloke replied, 'That's Michelle.'
(me shell)

What did the coat hanger say to the shirt?

'Do you have to hang around me all day?'

What do you call a computer superhero?

A screensaver!

Attending a wedding for the first time, a little girl whispered to her mother, 'Why is the bride dressed in white?'

'Because white is the colour of happiness and today is the happiest day of her life.'

The child thought about this for a moment and then said, 'So why is the groom wearing black?'

David Koch—presenter, Sunrise

CELEBRITY CRACK-UPS!

What do you call a pile of writing paper that doesn't move?

Stationary stationery.

What do trees drink?

Root beer.

What do you call a bloke who is
always stealing things?

Rob.

Why did the cops wake up the sleeping child?

They heard that there was a kid napping!

What happened when the police found Keith, the
little lost boy, hiding under a blanket?

There was a cover-up.

How did little Johnny feel about
his mother having his undies made?

Undismayed.

Pessimist: 'My glass is half empty.'

Optimist: 'My glass is half full.'

Detective: 'Dust that glass for prints
and find out who's been drinking my tea!'

What did the tie say to the shirt?

'Do you mind if I hang around?'

What did the shirt say to the tie?

'Get knotted!'

Why was the hand in jail?

It was under a wrist.

Did you hear about the prisoner who was keen
on grammar?

She was given a very long sentence.

Why didn't the fog get the joke?

It was too thick.

Why was the fog sad to be leaving?

It knew it would be mist.

Did the wind pass its exam?

Yes. It was a breeze.

What colour answers the phone?

Yellow.

Why did Kelly dream she was a tree?

She slept like a log.

Why does Edward Woodward have four
Ds in his name?

Otherwise his name would be Ewar
Woowar.

*Wil Anderson—comedian,
TV host and writer*

Can a match box?

No, but a tin can!

What simple card game can you play while asleep?

Nap!

Why did the shop owner go to karate classes?

She wanted to learn shelf-defence.

Do pieces of string have bad dreams?

Yes. They have knotmares.

Why did Jake always go to bed wearing a nappy?

So that he slept like a baby.

**Why was Jake's nappy-wearing
habit never found out?**

There was a big cover up.

Why did Jake wish he was taller?

So he could stay in bed longer.

What do you call an igloo without a toilet?

An ig.

**What happened when the cyclone and the gale
had a fight?**

They exchanged blows then it all blew over.

What do you call two criminals robbing
a house?

A pair of knickers.

Why did the bike just sit there?

It was two tyred.

What do you call a dream that involves
a mozzie attack?

A bitemare.

Why was the orange released from prison?

It was freed on a peel.

What did the shoe say to the sock?

'Hop in!'

What has eyes that cannot see, a tongue that cannot taste, and a soul that cannot die?

A shoe!

Two antennas met on a roof, fell in love and got married. The ceremony wasn't much, but the reception was excellent.

What do you call a woman with one leg?

Eileen.

FUNNY BUSINESS

How do you join the Australian Navy?

Handcuff all the sailors together.

Why are computers always so tired when they get home?

Because they all have hard drives!

What's the difference between an Australian lighthouse keeper, a watch-maker and a tube of superglue?

One watches the seas and the other sees the watches.

What about the tube of superglue?

Well, that's where you get stuck!

Why did the outback weatherman quit?

Because the climate didn't agree with him!

What's the difference between Dazza the jeweller and Bazza the jailer?

One sells watches and the other watches cells!

Did you hear about the octopus that became a soldier?

It was well-armed.

What was the newspaper headline following the short fortune-teller's escape from prison?

'Small medium at large.'

Did the fingers and thumb agree to work together?

Yes, and they made a good fist of things.

Have the elbows and knees agreed to work together?

Yes, it's going to be a joint effort.

One day Bazza decides that he's had enough of working and decides to become a thief. He goes out and snatches a purse from the first lady he sees. Unfortunately, Bazza is so dim that he does it in front of a policeman and the cop chases him. Bazza runs away down an alley and the policeman follows. At the end of the alley the policeman sees that it is a dead end and there is nothing there but three large sacks. 'That Bazza must be hiding in one of them', thinks the policeman and pokes the first sack with his boot.

'Grr-Woof!' comes a noise from the sack. There is a dog hiding inside.

'Meee-oww!' comes the noise from the second sack. 'Cats', thinks the policeman. He moves on to the third sack and pokes it with his boot.

At first, there is silence. Then, 'Aaah . . . umm . . . potatoes?'

'My barber has invented a fantastic machine,' a man told his friend. 'You stick your head in and it shaves you in a matter of seconds.'

'That's impossible,' declared the friend. 'Everyone's head is shaped differently.' 'Sure,' said the first man, 'but only at first!'

Andy Griffiths—children's author

CELEBRITY CRACK-UPS!

What happened to the Aussie who cleaned the chimney in the clothing factory?

He got covered in suit.

Did you hear about the spy whose bedspread blew off the washing line?

His cover was blown.

Spy boss: 'Agent 011, why were you gluing feathers to the suspect's bottom?'

Agent 011: 'You told me to tail him, sir.'

Spy boss: 'Agent 012, why did you refuse to get out of bed?'

Agent 012: 'You told me to stay under cover, sir.'

Spy boss: 'Agent 013, why didn't you examine the suspect's suitcase?'

Agent 013: 'You told me the case was closed, sir.'

Spy boss: 'Agent 014, I've got the code!'

Agent 014: 'Sorry to hear it, sir. I hope you get better soon.'

Spy boss: 'Agent 015, why do you insist on drinking out of black tumblers?'

Agent 015: 'I always use dark glasses, sir.'

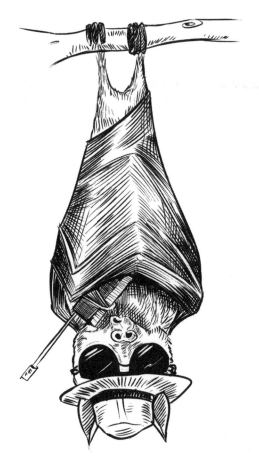

Spy boss: 'Agent 016, why do you always sit at the counter at the local café?'

Agent 016: 'You told me to concentrate on counterintelligence, sir.'

Spy boss: 'Agent 017, from now on you'll operate as a double agent.'

Agent 017: 'What if I get caught, sir?'

Spy boss: 'I'll deny any knowledge of either of you.'

Why do spies hate polka-dot shirts?

They don't like to be spotted.

What do magicians like to keep up their sleeves?

Their arms!

Why did the arm ask for help?

It needed a hand.

Did the feet agree to work together?

Well, there were toes that did and there were toes that didn't.

A doctor, a lawyer and an accountant walk
into a restaurant and the waiter says,
'What is this? A joke?'

Did you hear about the angry clothes shop manager?

He got shirty.

Why was the tightrope walker so successful?

She was a well-balanced individual.

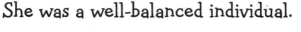

Did you hear about the ambitious torso?

It was determined to get ahead.

**How did the computer programmer
look after her lawns?**

She modem.

Why were the queen's subjects soaking wet?

She was the raining monarch.

How did the computer programmer dry her clothes?

She put them on line.

Did you hear about the net surfer who laughed and laughed and laughed?

She got a fit of the Googles.

Keith: 'What's the lowest rank in the army?'

Brett: 'I'm not telling you. It's private.'

Why did the soldier rush to clean his boots?

He stepped into the officers' mess.

Did you hear about the trapeze artists
who got married?

They fell for each other on the net.

What's being done about the gaping hole that
appeared overnight in the prison wall?

The police are looking into it.

Why did the comedian go to sewing classes?

He planned to have his audience in stitches.

What happened to the computer programmer who
was attacked by a giant mosquito?

She copped a megabyte.

Why was the computer salesman
so comfortable in his clothes?

He specialised in softwear.

Did you hear about the prisoner
who stuck to the rules?

She got time off for glued behaviour.

Why was the broom late for work?

It over-swept.

Why did the jockey practise sprinting
to his mailbox?

He was always desperate to be first to the post.

Why did the gunslinger carry a pencil and paper?

So he could be quick on the draw.

What do you call a man doing housekeeping?

Cinderfella!

Why did the projectionist cross the road?

To get to the other slide.

What do you call a nun with a washing machine on her head?

Sister matic.

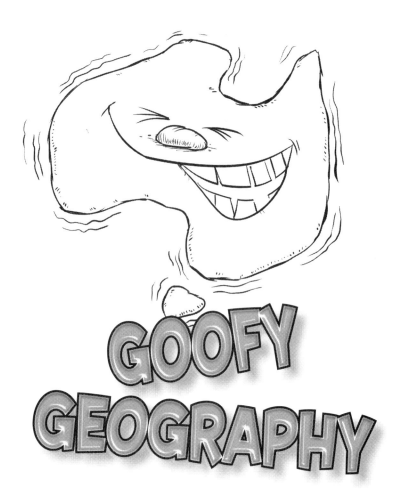

GOOFY GEOGRAPHY

What kind of letters do you send to the
Australian capital city?

Capital letters.

What did the volcano say to his girlfriend?

I lava you.

What do you call a chicken in Antarctica?

Lost!

What else do you call a chicken
in Antarctica?

Cold!

Danny: 'I took my wife on holiday to the Caribbean.'

Ryan: 'Jamaica?'

Danny: 'No, she wanted to go!'

Simmo: 'Our new neighbours are Irish! '

Ben: 'Oh, really?'

Simmo: 'No, O'Reilly.'

Which country eats the most tinned fruit?

Can-ada!

There are two snowmen standing on a hill.
One turns to the other and says, 'Say, do you
smell carrots?'

Which country has the chilliest people?

Brrrrrazil!

Does New Zealand get lots of rain?

Yes, there's absolutely no drought about it.

Which country has the most microbes?

Germ-any!

**Which country is the best at
board games?**

Checkerslovakia!

Which country is always dressed nicely?

Tie-land!

Which country has the worst singers?

Sing-a-poor!

If a green bloke runs over the Blue Mountains,
what does he become?

Tired!

Keith Koala: 'Where are the Blue Mountains?'

Wally Wombat: 'I don't know and
I don't have them I swear!'

What's the capital of Australia?

A.

Where in Australasia would you
find herds of wildebeest?

Gnu Zealand.

Which country has the most church bells?

Bell-gium!

What's the smartest mountain in the world?

Mount Cleverest.

Why can't Egyptian swimmers face up to the truth?

They're mostly in de Nile.

Why are Spanish aircraft always wet?

The rain in Spain falls mainly on the plane.

**Did you hear the joke about the Eskimo
at the North Pole?**

Don't worry; it would chill you to the bone!

**What did the Aussie tourist say to the
Eskimo about his new igloo?**

That's an ice house you have there!

What is the best thing to take into
the Simpson Desert?

A thirst-aid kit!

How did an Irish city suddenly manage to produce
twice its number of citizens?

By Dublin its population.

What travels around the world and stays
in the corner?

A stamp.

Around which sea is there a lot of muddy terrain?

The Muddyterrainean Sea.

Which country is famous for
its chocolates and desserts?

Sweetzerland.

Where do swings come from?

Swingapore.

What's in the middle of Paris?

The letter 'r'.

Where do parkas come from?

Parkastan.

What if London were flooded by
its river?

Thames the breaks.

Where do bangles come from?

Bangle-adesh.

Where do balls come from?

Ballivia.

Where are the Andes?

At the end of your armies.

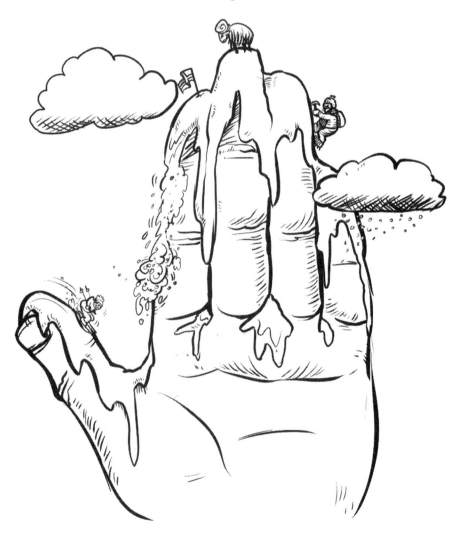

Why does everyone love Antarctica?

It's just so cool!

Is it possible to build a road in Antarctica?

Snow way.

Where does jam come from?

Jam-maker.

What is a Fjord?

A Norwegian car.

Where do boots come from?

Bootswana.

Where do car horns come from?

Honk Kong.

Where do hire cars come from?

Hireland.

Where do circus clowns come from?

Completelymadagascar.

Where do nutcrackers come from?

Crushia.

Where do snooker cues come from?

Snookercuba.

Where do pans come from?

Panama.

Where do knickers come from?

Knickeragua.

Where do columns come from?

Columnbia.

Where do corks come from?

The Corkney Islands.

Where do crows come from?

Crowatia.

Where do barges come from?

Bargentina.

What would happen to the passengers
of a Paris bus if it toppled
into the river?

They'd all be driven in Seine.

SIDE-SPLITTING SCARES

How do you make a witch itch?

Take away the W.

What kind of ape likes Australian
horror movies?

A gore-illa.

How do ghosts style their hair?

With scarespray.

On which day did the bloke turn into a werewolf?

Moonday.

On which day did the werewolf start eating people?

Chewsday.

On which day did the werewolf turn back
into a bloke?

Mensday.

On which day did the bloke find hair everywhere
from when he was a werewolf?

Fursday.

On which day did the bloke decide to have bacon
and eggs instead of becoming a werewolf again?

Fryday!

How do ghosts like their eggs in the morning?

Terri-fried!

What's a ghost's favourite musical?

My Fear Lady.

Which dinosaur stayed in the rain for too long?

Brontosau-rust.

What do you call a vampire who lives in your
kitchen utensils drawer?

Count Spatula!

What do you get when you cross a duck
with a vampire?

Count Quackular!

What do you get when you cross a teacher
with a vampire?

Lots of blood tests!

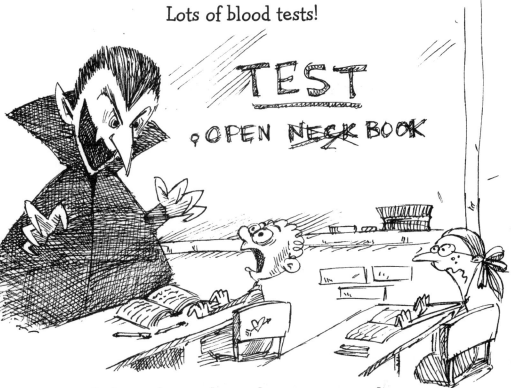

Did you hear about the magician who
disappeared on his morning walk?

He turned into a laneway.

Why did the pilot scream in terror?

He got a terrible flight.

How do witches get to a wedding?

On the groom.

What did Kylie the skeleton say to the other skeleton before dinner?

'Bone appétit!'

Why did Bluey the skeleton go to the music shop?

To get the new organ.

Why did the priest take the ghost for a walk?

He was asked to exorcise it.

What is a ghost's favourite animal?

A night-mare!

What is Dracula's favourite type of dog?

A bloodhound.

What are a ghost's scariest camp-fire stories?

Human stories!

What kind of dog is the scariest?

The terror-ier.

What are the symptoms of a vampire's flu?

Lots of coffin.

What do you get if you cross a phone with a ghost?

A phantom phone booth.

What do you get if you cross a dinosaur
with a ghost?

A boo-saurus.

What do you get if you cross
a ghost with a vacuum-cleaner?

A howler!

What do you get when you cross
a werewolf with a dozen eggs?

A very hairy omelette.

What should you do if Frankenstein's monster approaches you?

Make a bolt for it.

Why did the chicken go to the seance?

To get to the other side.

Andrew Daddo—television presenter and author

CELEBRITY CRACK-UPS!

What do near-sighted ghosts use to read?

Spookticles.

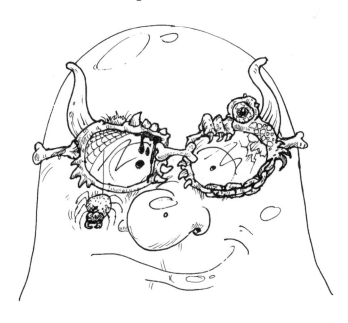

Why do zombies from all over the city meet at the cemetery?

It's the dead centre of town.

Why is Count Dracula easily fooled?

He's a real sucker.

When a werewolf gets lost, what does it become?

A wherewolf.

Why didn't the skeleton go to the party?

Because it had no body to go with.

Where do the spooks of NSW hold their get-togethers?

Ghoulburn.

Why did the skeleton visit the restaurant?

It wanted some spare ribs.

Which monster likes to officiate at cricket matches?

A vumpire.

What do you get when you cross a snowman
and a vampire?

Frostbite.

Why couldn't the Invisible Man
fool anyone?

People could see through him.

Why was the skeleton afraid to jump off the
Sydney Harbour Bridge?

Because it didn't have any guts.

What do you get when King Kong appears?

Out of his way.

Where do Aussie witches learn to fly?

Broome.

What do you call a skeleton that rings your doorbell?

A dead ringer.

What type of girls does a vampire like?

Red heads.

Which monster roams the Himalayas, firing arrows at anyone it sees?

The Abominable Bowman.

What's a monster's favourite bean?

A human bean.

What do you get when you cross a
fortune-teller with a gardener?

Someone who can weed palms!

What do Italian ghosts have for dinner?

Spookhetti!

What kind of cake do you eat at a
horror movie?

I scream cake.

What did the alien say to the garden?

'Take me to your weeder!'

Why was 6 scared?

Because 7 8 9 (7 ate 9).

What's a witch's favourite computer program?

The spell checker.

What do gnomes do after school?

Gnome work.

CLASSROOM CRACK-UPS

Why was the teacher cross-eyed?

Because she couldn't control her pupils!

Alinta Manasserian—Presenter, Totally Wild

CELEBRITY CRACK-UPS!

Where do cows go to study?

Moo-niversity.

What's the friendliest school?

Hi school.

What do you call that great feeling of satisfaction
you get when you finish your homework?

The aftermath.

What happened to Ellie Emu's lunch money?

She ate it, of course!

Twelve people were under the same umbrella.
How come nobody got wet?

Because it wasn't raining.

What kind of school do you have to drop out of to graduate?

Sky-diving school.

Teacher: 'Johnny, if you had five chocolate bars and Stevie asked for two, how many would you have left?'

Johnny: 'Five.'

Which is the best hand to write with?

It's probably better to write with a pen.

What 11-letter word does everybody always pronounce incorrectly?

Incorrectly.

A Year Five class goes on an excursion to Taronga Zoo and they get to ride the ferry across Sydney Harbour. Before they are allowed onboard, the teacher gives everyone a talk on the safety rules. She is sure everyone will be safe except for Naughty Nigel, who has been mucking around through the entire safety lecture.

'Nigel!' yells the teacher. 'This is very important! What do you yell if you see one of your fellow students go over the side of the boat?'

To the teacher's surprise, Nigel replies 'Man overboard!'

'Okay then,' says the teacher, suspecting a lucky guess. 'What do you yell if your teacher goes over the side of the boat?'

'Hooray!'

Who is Katey Kangaroo's best friend at school?

Her princi-pal.

There was once an inflatable boy who went to an inflatable school. All the buildings were inflatable, and the teachers were inflatable, even the other students were inflatable. One day the boy got in trouble for bringing a pin to school and was called into the principal's office. The principal glared at him and said, 'You've let me down, you've let yourself down, you've let the whole school down.'

Adam Hills—comedian and presenter

Teacher: 'Marc, give me a sentence starting with the letter 'I'.'

Marc: 'I is . . .'

Teacher: 'No, Marc. It's 'I am', not 'I is'. Try again.'

Marc: 'Okay. I am the ninth letter of the alphabet.'

What made Keith Koala go around and around and around and around and around the playground?

He lost his marbles!

Wally Wombat: 'Why did you bring your computer to school, Keith?'

Keith Koala: 'My mum told me to bring an apple for Miss Smith!'

Why did Wally Wombat give Ellie Emu a kitten treat?

Because Ellie is the teacher's pet!

Why did Keith Koala give the teacher a C sharp?

It was a note from his parents!

Why did Ellie Emu use hair gel before
a swimming race?

She wanted to be the slipperiest!

What did Katey Kangaroo's maths book say to Ellie
Emu's maths book?

I have *so* many problems!

Keith Koala: 'How did you go in your test?'

Patty Platypus: 'Well, it was watery.'

Keith Koala: 'What do you mean?'

Patty Platypus: 'My results were under
C level!'

Ellie Emu: 'I didn't understand that test!
Why were all the questions from before I was born?'

Keith Koala: 'It was a history test . . .'

Ellie Emu stands in front of her classmates, giving a monologue on her love of knowledge. 'I love learning. It is so rewarding. I love to know what makes things work. I thirst for understanding as if my lips are dry and my tongue is swollen . . .'

Meanwhile, Wally Wombat is frantically waving his arms at her, trying to interrupt, with a worried expression. Finally he gets Ellie's attention and he hands her something.

'What's this?' Ellie queries.

Wally says: 'It's a glass of water for your thirst!'

Teacher: 'How many sides does Katey Kangaroo's pouch have?'

Class: 'Two—the inside and the outside!'

Teacher: 'Katey Kangaroo, do you know when the great depression was?'

Katey Kangaroo: 'Yes, when I got my last haircut!'

Teacher: 'What is that tree in the playground, Keith Koala?'

Keith Koala: 'An elemen-tree!'

Teacher: 'What's that sound I can hear from the gym? It sounds like music.'

Katey Kangaroo: 'The sports teacher told Keith to go get a ball. Guess Keith thought he meant the dancing kind!'

What kind of bee loves going to school?

A spelling bee.

What kind of school do magicians go to?

Charm school!

What sort of end-of-school dance to rabbits go to?

A hare-ball.

What did the kid say when the teacher asked who kept putting boogers on her chair?

S'not me!

What bird loves singing class?

A hummingbird.

Teacher: 'Tanya. "Woolloomooloo"–spell it.'

Tanya: 'Umm...I-T...'

Teacher: 'Keanu, how do you spell "Woolloomooloo"?'

Keanu: 'I don't.'

Teacher: 'How did you find the exam questions, Carly?'

Carly: 'Easy. I walked into the exam room and there they were.'

When a teacher closes his eyes, why should it remind him of an empty classroom?

Because there are no pupils to see!

Teacher: 'Johnno, it's clear that you haven't studied your geography. What's your excuse?'

Johnno: 'Well, my dad says the world is changing every day. So I decided to wait until it settles down!'

Father: 'How do you like going to school?'

Son: 'The going bit is fine, the coming home bit too . . . but I'm not too keen on the time in-between!'

Teacher: 'How did you find the exam questions, Helen?'

Helen: 'The questions were easy. It was the answers I had trouble with.'

Is it true that Albert doesn't like school?

It's not really school he dislikes, it's the principal of the thing.

Teacher: 'Nicole, name three different Australian marsupials.'

Nicole: 'A mother koala, a father koala and a baby koala.'

Teacher: 'Noni, give me an example of a word that can be a noun or a verb.'

Noni: 'Pardon?'

Teacher: 'Correct.'

ANIMAL WISEQUACKS

Which shark would be useful in retirement homes?

The grey nurse.

Why couldn't Bruce tell what was
around his dog Max's neck?

He was collar blind.

How many skunks does it take to make a big stink?

A phew.

Why did the joke make the rabbit laugh?

It was hilariously bunny.

What do you call a story about a hairy
little horse?

A ponytale.

Did you hear about the prankster who pretended
he'd found a bird's wing?

It was just a bit of a lark.

Did you hear about the embarrassed gander?

It felt like a goose.

Why were the eagle chicks nervous in their nest?

It just felt so eyrie.

Where do steers go for their morning coffee?

The nearest bullbar.

Why did the gaming police raid the farm?

They heard that lambs were gambolling in the fields.

Did you hear about the lonely drake that was hopeless at cricket?

It was out for a duck.

How did the shepherdess get dressed up for the party?

She wore her best flock.

Did you hear about the tall bird that acted crazy?

It went stork raving mad.

What happened at the wasps' annual get-together?

They gathered round the piano and had a sting-along.

What did the wasp say to the bee?

'Hey honey, what's the buzz?'

What sheep never fails to open doors?

A battering ram.

What did the bee say to the wasp?

'Don't bug me! Hive had enough!'

What do you get when you cross
a cockatoo with a poodle?

A cocka-poodle-doo!

What loves Santa and looks like a Volkswagen?

A Christmas beetle.

What has fifty legs and can't walk?

Half a centipede.

Why was the margarine jealous?

It saw the butter fly.

Which dogs are very quiet and are always at your feet?

Hush puppies.

Why do cows have bells around their necks?

Because their horns don't work!

What if pigs could fly?

Bacon would go up.

How did the ants make a fire at their bush camp?

They rubbed two stick insects together.

What is a snail?

A slug with a crash helmet on.

What do you call a three-legged donkey?

A wonkey!

Did you hear about the amusing duck?

It quacked a joke.

Did the other ducks like the joke?

They quacked up.

Did you hear about the cannibal duck?

It ate a quacker.

What do ducklings hope to achieve at their local primary?

They aim to be dux of the school.

What did the horse dance at the wedding?

The bridle waltz.

What do you call a border collie crossed
with a flower?

A collie flower.

Did you hear about the tortoise that conquered
its shyness?

It came out of its shell.

When is it bad luck to be followed by a black cat?

When you're a mouse.

What goes tick tick woof?

A watchdog.

Did you hear about the dog that ran
around the oval all day?

It was a lapdog.

Why do dogs have flat noses?

They keep running into parked cars!

What do you call a cat that likes digging
in the dirt?

A bob cat.

What time is it when an elephant sits on your fence?

Time to get a new fence.

What do cows watch on TV?

Mooooovies.

Omar: 'My dog has no nose.'

Jenny: 'How does he smell?'

Omar: 'Really bad.'

How did Kylie know her pet was just an average, everyday cat?

It was just a feline she had.

There are two goldfish in a tank. One turns to the other and asks, 'Do you know how to drive this thing?'

What happened when the nocturnal birds were woken during daylight hours?

There were owls of protest.

What do you call a sleeping bull?

A bulldozer.

What did the farmer say when he had gathered all his animals together?

'Now I've herd everything.'

Which species of turtle is always ready for an argument?

Loggerhead.

Why can't leopards hide?

Because you can spot them.

What's black, white and red all over?

A newspaper—or a penguin with a nosebleed!

What's black, white and red all over?

An embarrassed zebra.

Where would you find a large black bird
on lookout duty?

The crow's nest.

Which circus animals are the most popular?

The lions are the mane attraction.

Why did the dog ride into town with a murderous
look in his eye?

He was looking for the man that shot his paw.

FAIR-DINKUM FAMOUS

Who is a pig's favourite superhero?

The Oinkredible Hulk.

Who writes books about curries?

Roald Dahl.

What's Winnie the Pooh's middle name?

The.

What's the easiest way to get on Australian TV?

Sit next to the aerial!

Who wears blue tights, a red cape and smells like
pea and ham?

Souperman!

Why is Cinderella so bad at soccer?

She keeps running away from the ball!

How does the Easter Bunny stay so fit?

He gets lots of eggs-ercise with hare-obics

Which famous general enjoyed playground games?

Handball the Great!

Which great French military leader fell to bits?

Napoleon Bones-apart!

What did the man say when he looked at the Mona Lisa?

'Aha, I get the picture…'

Knock knock!

Who's there?

Doctor.

Doctor who?

How did you know?

Which famous pharaoh was seriously overweight?

Two-Tonne Carmen.

What do you call James Bond in the bath?

Bubble-0-7!

Which Scot invented the steam engine?

Watt.

Which Scot invented the steam engine?

Watt.

ARE YOU LISTENING TO ME?
WHICH SCOT INVENTED THE STEAM ENGINE?

Watt!

Which famous queen suffered badly from measles?

Mary, Queen of Spots!

What do you get when you put hot water down a rabbit hole?

Hot cross bunnies.

Do Santa's reindeer enjoy his jokes?

Yes. He sleighs 'em.

Which Australian poet was highly strung?

Banjo Paterson.

In Santa's sleigh team, who is the most ill-mannered?

Rude Alf, the red-nosed reindeer.

Why is there never a drought where Santa lives?

There's always plenty of rain, dear.

How does Santa stop his sleigh?

He just pulls on the rein, dear.

Does Santa enjoy being king of the North Pole?

Yes, he likes his reign, dear.

Which famous movies involve lots of climbing?

Lord of the Rungs and Stair Wars.

Which Wild West hero had a throat
spasm problem?

Wild Bill Hiccup.

Which Wild West outlaw was a bit of a goat?

Billy the Kid.

Which Wild West frontiersman had a very short hairstyle?

Davy Crewcut.

Did Moby Dick enjoy the party?

He had a whale of a time.

Why did Tigger look inside the toilet?

Because he was looking for Pooh!

What is the name of the fishy spy?

James Pond.

Which vegetable became a rock' n 'roll superstar?

Elvis Parsley.

Which outlaw developed a famous breed of sheepdog?

Ned Collie.

Which famous philosopher loved French fries?

Plato Chips!

Did you hear about the fairy godmother
who couldn't spell?

She turned a handsome prince into a forg.

Which authors of fairytales were always in trouble
with the police?

The Brothers Crim.

A pig walks into a bar and asks for fifty glasses of
water. When he finishes drinking them,
the barkeeper asks, 'Don't you need to go to
the toilet now?'

'No,' replies the pig, 'because I go wee wee wee
all the way home.'

Which fairytale involves piglets hanging
out the washing?

The Three Little Pegs.

Which favourite jumbo got stuck in a swamp?

The Soggy Boggy Elephant.

What's E.T. short for?

He's only got little legs.

Who is a nose's favourite wizard?

Harry Snotter.

Who invented the ship's oven?

Captain James Cooker.

Who invented the ancient Roman icebox?

Julius Freezer.

Which movie star invented a golf stroke?

Brad Putt.

Which famous motor engineer invented the
Norwegian coastline?

Henry Fjord.

Which African leader invented a mystic symbol
of the universe?

Nelson Mandala.

What did Santa say to the cowboy?

'Let's have a ho-down.'

In which fairytale does a young boy have a long
chat to some vegetables?

Jack and the Beans Talk.

What lovely little shoe fell under a spell and was doomed to sleep forever?

Sleeping Bootie.

Who was the bad-mannered little girl who went off to visit her grandma?

Little Rude Riding Hood.

In which fairytale does a young girl gobble
up horses' breakfasts?

Goldilocks and the Three Mares.

Which fairytale tells of a young royal who takes
her dog for a walk and cleans up the messes
it makes?

The Pooper Bag Princess.

Which fairytale tells of a young royal's
visit to the toilet?

The Princess and the Pee.

TRANSPORT TRIP-UPS

How did the car get a flat tyre?

There was a fork in the road.

What happened to the wooden car with the wooden engine and wooden tyres?

It wooden go.

What do you call music coming out of a car?

A cartune!

Did you hear about the bus driver who was arrested
on a cattle station?

He was charged with dangerous droving.

How does the queen get around her palace?

She's throne.

Did you hear about the magic car?

It turned into a driveway.

What do monsters make with cars?

A traffic jam.

How do Aussie pilots undress for bed?

They prepare for take-off.

Where does the HMAS Mouse tie up
when in port?

The Hickory Dickory Dock.

What's the last thing that goes through a bee's mind when he hits the windshield?

His bottom!

What kind of emu can stop traffic?

A policemun.

What do bees do if they don't want to drive?

Go to the buzz stop.

How do rabbits fly?

By hare plane.

Why can't penguins fly?

Because plane tickets are really expensive!

What did the traffic light say to the other traffic light?

Excuse me, I'm changing.

Two police officers are driving a car. One officer puts on the siren and asks the other officer to check whether it's working. He answers 'Yes . . . no . . . yes . . . no . . . yes . . . no . . . yes . . . no . . .'

Luke Mangan—celebrity chef

CELEBRITY CRACK-UPS!

A peanut sat on a railway track
His heart was a flutter
Along came the 6.15
Toot toot, peanut butter!

What flies and wobbles?

A jellycopter.

Katey Kangaroo: 'Keith! Call me a taxi!'

Keith: 'Certainly, Katey! You're a taxi!'

**What's the difference between a kangaroo
and a train carriage?**

Well if you can't tell the difference,
I'm not going to try to explain it!

**What did the dog say as it admired the front
of the big ship?**

Bow! Wow!

Where does an elephant keep its luggage?

In its trunk.

What price would a baby magpie buy a sports car for?

Cheep cheep!

What happens when a cane toad breaks down?

It gets toad away.

Why did the commuter refuse to pay for
her bus journey?

She felt it just wasn't fare.

Why did the stair builder become an excellent pilot?

He made perfect landings.

Why did the poor fisherman fail as a pilot?

He couldn't land a thing.

Did you hear about the commuter who wrote
to ask for a tekcit?

She wanted a return ticket.

What language is spoken on all aircraft?

Plane English.

Where do wigs land and take off?

At hairports.

How did the fighter pilot get bitten?

He got involved in a dogfight.

Why was there panic at the airport?

There were jumbos everywhere.

Did you hear about the amazing magic bus?

It turned into a shopping centre.

Did you hear about the clumsy race mechanic who got covered in petrol?

He made a complete fuel of himself.

Was the new warplane design a success?

No, it bombed.

Did you hear about the racing car that needed a rest?

It was tyred and exhausted.

Why did the footy trainer fall over?

The players organised a coach trip.

Did the race mechanic enjoy his job?

No, he thought it was the pits.

Why was there absolutely nothing in the bus?

All the seats had been taken.

Why couldn't the bus play golf?

It didn't have a driver.

Why does a surfer meet passengers as they enter an aircraft?

To show them a board.

Did you hear about the bus tyre that didn't fulfil its potential?

It let itself down.

Why was the driver arrested after winning the race?

He took the chequered flag.

Why did the racing car go crazy?

It was being driven round the bend.

Why do racing drivers jump at the sound of a pistol?

It gives them a start.

**Did you hear about the weary driver
who couldn't stop in time?**

She was in need of a brake.

Why did the lights go out at the small racetrack?

There was a short circuit.

Why was the taxi covered in dents?

It kept getting hailed.

**Why did the driver stop and get into another
set of clothes?**

She decided to change gear.

What made the stop sign blush?

It saw the red light changing.

Did you hear about the angry driver who
had had enough?

He put his foot down.

Wayne: 'How long will the next bus be?'

Shane: 'Oh, about 11 metres.'

What is a bus drivers' meeting called?

A steering committee.

How do you know Aussie policemen are strong?

Because they can hold up traffic.

KNOCK KNOCKS

Knock, knock.
Who's there?
Amos.
Amos who?
Amossie just bit me!

Knock, knock.
Who's there?
Andy.
Andy who?
Andy just bit me again!

Knock, knock.
Who's there?
Howard.
Howard who?
Howard I know!

Knock, knock.
Who's there?
Archie!
Archie who?
Bless you!

Knock, knock.
Who's there?
Eileen.
Eileen who?
Eileen on you, you lean on me!

Knock, knock.
Who's there?
Emussen.
Emussen who?
Emussen run too fast or we'll lose him!

Knock, knock.
Who's there?
Robin.
Robin who?
**Robin you, so hand over
your money.**

Knock, knock.
Who's there?
Cargo.
Cargo who?
Cargo Beep Beep!

Knock, knock.
Who's there?
Hugo.
Hugo who?
Hugo this way, I go that way.

Knock, knock.
Who's there?
Grape.
Grape who?
It's grape to meet you.

Knock, knock.
Who's there?
Phillip.
Phillip who?
Phillip my lunch box, I'm hungry today!

Knock, knock.
Who's there?
Tomato.
Tomato who?
**Tomato from my knee, my plaster cast
is signed by the whole class!**

Knock, knock.
Who's there?
Doowie.
Doowie who?
Doowie have to go to school?

Knock, knock.
Who's there?
Doctor.
Doctor Who?
No, he's in the Tardis at the moment!

Would you miss me if I left tomorrow?
Yes.
Would you miss me if I left next week?
Yes.
Would you miss me if I left next year?
Yes.
Knock, knock.
Who's there?
Oh, you have forgotten me already!

Knock, knock.
Who's there? Cows go boo.
Cows go boo who?
I didn't know cows could cry.

Knock, knock.
Who's there?
Cow.
Cow who?
**Cows don't say who.
They say moo!**

Knock, knock.
Who's there?
Police.
Police who?
**Police don't tell my mum
I broke her vase!**

Knock, knock.
Who's there?
Lettuce.
Lettuce who?
**Lettuce come in to your party,
it's boring out here!**

Knock, knock!
Who's there?
Ivan.
Ivan who?
Ivan itchy nose.

Knock, knock.
Who's there?
Who.
Who who?
You're not an owl, are you?

Knock, knock!
Who's there?
Harriet.
Harriet who?
Harri-et's getting late.

Knock, knock!
Who's there?
Hiram.
Hiram who?
Hiram motorcycle for your trip.

Knock, knock!
Who's there?
Isabel.
Isabel who?
Isabel useful on a bicycle?

Knock, knock!
Who's there?
Woo.
Woo who?
Woo-hoo to you too!

Knock, knock!
Who's there?
Jim.
Jim who?
Jim mind if I keep that to myself?

Knock, knock!
Who's there?
Harry.
Harry who?
Harry up and open this door.

Knock, knock!
Who's there?
Ivor.
Ivor who?
Ivor get.

Knock, knock!
Who's there?
Carmen.
Carmen who?
Carmen see for yourself.

Knock, knock!
Who's there?
Mitchell.
Mitchell who?
Mitchell do for now.

Knock, knock!
Who's there?
Eva.
Eva who?
Eva brick through the window, and you'll see who.

Knock, knock!
Who's there?
Les.
Les who?
Les just stick to first names.

Knock, knock!
Who's there?
I'm Abby.
I'm Abby who?
I'm Abby to meet you.

Knock, knock!
Who's there?
Boo.
Boo who?
No need to cry about it.

Knock, knock!
Who's there?
Neil.
Neil who?
Neil down and peek through the keyhole.

Knock, knock!
Who's there?
Marion.
Marion who?
I'm not marryin' anyone—now let me in!

Knock, Knock!
Who's there?
Nobody!
Nobody who?
(Nobody says anything because there's nobody there.)

Knock, knock!
Who's there?
Stan.
Stan who?
Stan back—I'm comin' through!

Knock, knock!
Who's there?
Doris.
Doris who?
Doris locked—open up!

Knock, knock!
Who's there?
Will.
Will who?
Will you let me in? It's cold out here!

Knock, knock!
Who's there?
Ahmed.
Ahmed who?
Ahmed a mess on your doorstep.

Knock, knock!
Who's there?
Sonia.
Sonia who?
Sonia shoe, I can smell it from here!

Knock, knock!
Who's there?
Carl.
Carl who?
Carl the doctor—you must be deaf.

GROSS-OUT GROANERS

Why did the wombat bring toilet paper
to the party?

Because he was a party pooper!

Livinia Nixon—television presenter

**CELEBRITY
CRACK-UPS!**

What's green, sticky and smells like eucalyptus?

Koala spew.

If people point to their mouths when they're hungry and their wrists when they want the time, why don't they point to their bums when they need the bathroom?

What's green and hangs from tall trees?

Giraffe snot.

Which Australian city is the stinkiest?

Smellbourne!

Did you hear about the nose that was badly behaved?

It was very, very s'naughty.

If you're an Australian in the kitchen, an Australian in the lounge room and an Australian in the bathroom, what are you in the toilet?

European. (you're a peein')

Two blokes go into a hotel toilet. One is in the navy and the other is in the army. When they are done, the navy bloke goes to the sink and starts to wash his hands, while the army bloke goes to walk straight out the door.

The navy bloke calls after the army bloke, 'The navy teaches us to wash our hands!'

The army bloke calls back, 'The army teaches us not to pee on ours!'

Which big animal needs a bath?

A smellyphant.

What do you call a smelly fairy?

Stinkerbell.

What's a face race?

It's a feature race.

Is the face race a new idea?

No, it's been happening for ears and ears.

What's the face race distance?

Half a smile (2 lips of the oval).

Did Jack enter the face race?

Yes, his nose was running.

Did Jill enter the face race?

Yes, her eyes were running.

Why was Jack disqualified from the face race?

He was too cheeky.

Was Jack upset?

No, he took it on the chin.

Who won the face race?

Jill. She was blinking fast.

Will the race continue?

Definitely! There will be lots of new faces next year.

Will Jack compete again next year?

Who nose?

Why do gorillas have big noses?

Because they have big fingers.

What did the lazy right hand think to itself?

'I'd better knuckle down.'

What did the lazy left hand think to itself?

'I'd better get a grip.'

What do your hands need so they can
visit your arms?

Two-wrist visas.

What plant grows on your hand?

A palm.

Do hands enjoy life?

Thumb do and thumb don't.

What did the finger say to the thumb?

'I'm in glove with you.'

What's invisible and smells like chocolate?

Easter Bunny farts!

How can you tell when a moth farts?

It flies straight for a second.

What's invisible, noisy and smells like bananas?

A monkey burp!

How many frogs would fit in your glass of water?

Toadily too many.

Two cows are standing in a field. One cow asks the other, 'Are you worried about this mad cow disease?' The other cow answers, 'Nah, us penguins can't catch it.'

Why did the patient think the surgeon was hilarious?

She had him in stitches.

Why did Kel, the nervous carpenter,
have broken teeth?

He was always biting his nails.

How do you get a tissue to dance?

Put a little boogie in it.

Did you hear about the court jester who was
ill then got better?

He made a fool recovery.

Why did the one-handed person cross the road?

To get to the second-hand shop.

What do you get if you eat tinsel?

Tinselitus!

What's the difference between flies and cockroaches?

Flies are easier to get out from between your teeth.

Why did the hand feel safe in a glove?

It was out of arm's way.

Why are hippies so useful?

Because they help swing your leggies!

What should you do if you get swallowed
by an elephant?

Jump up and down until you are all pooped out.

What monster gorilla farts a lot?

King Pong.

What children's game do farters love to play?

Hide-and-reek.

What sound do you hear when a cat gets run over by a lawn-mower?

MeeeOOWWW!

Why did Matt fart at Pat?

He odour one.

What does the legless man do all day?

He just bums around.

What does the armless man do all day?

Who cares? He's 'armless.

What favourite hero farts a lot?

Captain Thunderpants.

Three kids found a magic slide with a sign beside it which read: 'All riders will get what they wish for!' The first kid went down and said 'Cash!' and landed in a huge pile of money. The second kid went down and said 'Chocolate!' and landed in a mountain of chocolate bars. The third kid went down and said 'Weeeeee...'

What's yellow and sticky, smells of bananas, and lies on the forest floor?

Monkey vomit.

Why does Ping the table tennis player avoid eating baked beans?

They make Ping pong.

Why did Angie have a scorched bottom?

She tried on a pair of hot pants.

What use is your bottom in an orchestra?

It can function as a wind instrument.

What did the umpire say when the batsman farted?

'That's out!'

Where do pirates go to the toilet?

On the poop deck.

WET 'N' WILD

Where did the young river fish try to get a job?

At the bank.

Why did the ship's crew hear lots and lots of whistling?

They were sailing through lark-infested waters.

Why was the captain studying the menu?

He was deciding on his next course.

Why couldn't the captain work out his ship's speed?

He always got tangled in knots.

Was the cabin boy punished for slacking off
at the back of the ship?

No, but he was given a stern warning.

How did the Turkish ship remain in the one spot overnight?

It dropped Ankara.

Why was the angler hungry?

He didn't have a bite all day.

What was the angler's name?

Rod.

What do you call someone swimming in the middle of the Pacific Ocean?

Shark bait.

Was it really that easy to move the huge liner away from the dock?

Yes. It took only two little tugs on the ropes.

Why did the river get a shock?

The current got switched on.

How did the ship sail after the successful mutiny?

It was in crew's control.

How are rivers able to put the past behind them?

They see it as water under the bridge.

Why don't sharks eat clown fish?

Because they taste funny.

**A boy on a river bank yells to a boy
on the other bank:**

'How do I get to the other side?'

**The second boy calls back: 'You are on
the other side.'**

How do we know that fish are keen on education?

Most of them spend their lives in a school.

Did you hear about the romantic boy fish?

He just loved gills.

Did you hear about the romantic girl fish?

She just loved buoys.

Did you hear about the happy-go-lucky fish?

It just went with the flow.

Why was the flathead unhappy?

It wanted a mullet.

Is that fish a bit deaf?

Yes, it's very hard of herring.

What do you call a big white whale with wings
and a beak?

Moby Duck.

What key do whales sing in?

Sea.

What do you call a snail on a ship?

A snailor.

Why did the surfer lose interest?

He was in bored shorts.

What do upset whales do?

Blubber.

A group of passengers on a cruise ship can see a bearded man on a small island shouting and desperately waving his hands. 'Who is that?' a passenger asks the captain. The cruise ship captain replies, 'I've no idea. Every year when we pass, he goes nuts.'

Why is the sea friendly?

Because it waves!

What do you call a girl who lives at sea?

A sea-gal.

Did you hear about the boatman who tried to row along a dry stream bed?

He was up the creek without a puddle.

Why did the captain insist that two hands be on watch at all times?

He wanted one to be the big hand and one to be the little hand.

What do you call a fish without an eye?

A fsh.

What was all that commotion in the water?

There was something fishy going on.

What headgear was worn by the admiral in command of ten ships?

A 10-galleon hat.

Why was the sea roaring?

Because it had crabs on its bottom!

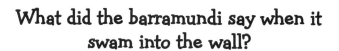

What did the barramundi say when it swam into the wall?

Dam!
Adam Cox—Presenter, Totally Wild
Dyan Blacklock—Author and Publisher

CELEBRITY CRACK-UPS!

What do you call a parrot with an umbrella?

Polly unsaturated.

OUTTA THIS WORLD!

How do you get an astronaut's baby to sleep?

Rock-it.

What did the hungry spaceman say to his co-pilot?

Pass the astronuts.

Wooooaaaaahhhhooooahaooow
(Translation: What do you do if you see a spaceman?)

You park in it man.

WALL.E.—(Disney PIXAR)

CELEBRITY CRACK-UPS!

Did you hear about Sharon, the astronomer who got knocked out?

She saw stars.

How do angels answer the phone?

Halo?

What do comets say when they are introduced to one another?

Nice to meteor!

What do Aussie astronauts do after a busy morning in space?

They go out to launch!

Why were the Aussie astronauts never around?

They kept going out to launch!

What do black holes eat for dinner?

Star-ghetti.

Why are there only 18 letters in the alphabet?

Because ET went home in a UFO and the CIA went after him!

What sort of dance do aliens do?

The moon walk!

Why was the alien cross?

Because he forgot change for the parking meteor!

Why was the alien afraid?

It was surrounded by shooting stars!

Why was the kangaroo on the red carpet?

Because it wanted to watch the stars come out.

What sort of gymnastics are aliens good at?

The moon beam!

Kangaroo: 'Why are you throwing vegetables in the sky, dear?'

Joey: 'Because I wanted to cook dinner for you in the big saucepan!'

Why wasn't the moon hungry?

Because it was full!

Which planet could you weave into an Aussie flag?

Saturn!

An atom walks into a bar and announces, 'I've lost an electron.' The barman asks, 'Are you sure?' The atom replies, 'I'm positive.'

Adam Spencer—radio presenter and comedian

When it landed in Sydney, why did the alien throw out all its clothes?

It was outer-space!

How do you know the sun is clean?

It always shines.

What did the Chinese astronauts cook their food in?

A space wok.

What did the first-time astronaut think of her trip into space?

She said it was out of this world.

What did the swim-crazy astronaut miss most about Earth?

The gravitational pool.

Why was the moon party dull?

Because it had no atmosphere!

How do astronauts take their tea?

The milky way.

Where did the astronaut catch the train?

At the space station.

What do you call silly spacemen?

Astronuts.

Did you hear about the astronaut who went crazy?

He went completely off the planet.

What star only comes out on Mondays?

A mon-star.

Why did the astronaut enjoy take-off so much?

She found it a real blast.

What did the alien say to the astronaut?

'Hello earthling, how on earth are you?'

Where did the crew of the space shuttle stop for a drink?

At a Mars bar.

JOKE-A-THON WINNERS!

One guy turns to another guy and says: 'It's raining cats and dogs outside.'

The other guy replies: 'I know. I just stepped in a poodle.'

Angela Caberica,
Joke-A-Thon winner

★

How do you send a centipede 100 feet in the air?

Turn it upside down.

Jeremy Wong,
Joke-A-Thon Winner

camp quality.

laughter is the best medicine.

With special thanks to contributors and supporters!

Thank you to all who helped with this book, for your hilarious jokes and support. A special thank-you to the many Australian children, celebrities and public for your contributions.

Noah Gray	Natasha Barrett	Courtney Whiteman
Theo Punkin	Jamie Hanrghan	Milind & Yash Bordia
Angela Rainbird	Adam Huxtable	Victoria Chhabra
Aiden O'Neill	Denver Sibary	Amy Wilson
Jordan Dixon	Bethany Clark	Rosalie He
Urgo Adem	Thea Ella McMahon	Zac Luimes
Baden Forster	Maddison Kosmac	Alexia Nikolovski
Charlie Southwell	Georgia Hope Robinson	Tamara Schiamn
William Cowiey	William Withers	Joe Spencer
Daniel Saunders	Scarlet Finn	Benjamin Bookworm
Blake	Anastasia Fiume	Chelsea Olafsen
Matthew	Patrick Gilmore	Ava Stroppiana
Angela Caberica	Rachael Foster	Chloe Thompson
Isobella	Marshall Blair	Callum Hemer
Marley	Deena Isles	Nicholis Mravicic
Apryl Mounsey	Jaden Victoria	Tarhlia Claydon
Riley Sawyer	Chloe Ann Gonano	Abby Claridge
Noah Butuyuyu	Mackenzie Gleeson	Leo Fyffe
Taylor	Indiana Gleeson	Sara Pascoe
Cooper Orendivk	Mahoney Gleeson	Candice Harding
Mikey McManus	Rachael Kent	Adhy Karina

Anders Wong

Anessa Karina

Brad Lester

Ciara Losty

Dylan McColl

Ella Guildea

Ewan Rule

Ganesh Owen Wilborn

Gitka McShane-Potts

Hayley Pepper

Heidi Bock

Josh Chagar

Jesse Chagar

Jim Dewar

Joanna Sterry

Josh Deathe

Liam Martin

Luke Addison

Max Everingham

Madison Campbell

Melina Karina

Michael Chalmers

Quinn Macdonald

Rachelle Gotz

Robyn Price

Sam Everingham

Tammie de Goede

Zac Goodall

Sally Baldwinson

Janne Banana

Zali Bell

Tahrin Bell

Len Bignell

Nicola Bignell

Christian Carbone

Sophie & Claudia Cassar

Zack Collins

Brianna Cooper

Rhys Cosgrave

Jacinta Cowin

Alana Dixon

Travis Dixon

Ashley Drake

Stephen & Sarah Dunkerley

MacKenzie Dunn

Paige Ellison

Paul Epthorp

Mark Frangie

Alexandra Goodenough

Pat Haynes

Caroline Hill

Eli Honner

Tom Hore

Courtney Hunt

Oliver Wright-Janoch

Annetta Jensen

Jin Jin

Jarrod Jones

Amanda Kirkham

Ally Moffett

Rachel Morell

Jessica Mulligan

Daniel O'Connell

Lachlan Oddie

Tony Park

Ana Patrocinio

Suzanne & Jessica Van Pelt

Powell Family

Tennille & Imogen Purton

Charlie Roberts

Connor Robertson

Tairi, Hemi and Taine Ruakere

Brittanie Seelenmeyer

Leukie Smith

Zac Smith

Shannedelle Stanley

Bethan Holloway-Strong

Nathan Szablewski

Marg Taft

Emily Walker

Lauren Whitton

Keith Wilson

Scott Woodward

Andy Yu

camp quality.

laughter is the best medicine.

Have you got a funny joke or game?

Send it to us and it might just end up being published in next year's joke book. How cool would that be?

Send it to us online now www.campquality.org.au/yourjoke

or write it down and post it.

**Camp Quality
My Joke
PO Box 400
Epping NSW 1710**

or tweet it to us and we might retweet it!
@camp_Quality, use #cqjoke

Name .... Age ....

Address ....

....

State .... Postcode ....

Phone ....

Email ....

My cool joke! ....

....

....

Would you like to help create a better life for every child living with cancer in Australia?

You can! Everyday, Camp Quality's kind supporters make a world of difference to the lives of children living with cancer and their families.

" The help you're giving is immeasurable" – a CQ Mum recently said, about our supporters.

Your donation allows us to deliver our programs to families when they need it most, building positivity and resilience that will benefit them throughout their lives.

Please make a donation today. It's easy!

complete and send the form on the bottom of this page.

Call us on 1300 662 267

Visit mycampquality.org.au/donate

Yes, I want to help create a better life for children living with cancer in Australia! 'Thanks so much for your kind support.'

My gift amount is: (please tick)

◯ $25   ◯ $50   ◯ Other

Gift Frequency:

◯ One-off   ◯ Monthly

My details are:

Title: . . . . . First name: . . . . Surname: . . . .

Address: . . . .

Suburb/Town: . . . . State: . . . . Postcode: . . . .

Phone/Mobile: . . . .

Email: . . . .

I wish to make my payment by:

◯ Cheque / Money Order   ◯ Mastercard   ◯ Visa   ◯ Amex

Card number: ◯◯◯◯ ◯◯◯◯ ◯◯◯◯ ◯◯◯◯

Expiry: ◯◯ / ◯◯   Name on card: . . . .

Your signature: . . . . Today's date: . . . .

Please return this completed form to:

Camp Quality, Reply Paid 400, Epping NSW 1710

or fax (02) 9869 0688 or call (02) 9876 0500 or donate online at

mycampquality.org.au/donate or email donorcare@campquality.org.au

All donations over $2 are tax deductible.

ABN 87 052 097 720

Would you like to help bring fun therapy to kids living with cancer?

Make a donation to bring happiness & optimism to children living with cancer & show that you believe laughter is the best medicine!

It's easy!
Donate to Camp Quality
in the following ways:
- Online: campquality.org.au
- By phone: 1300 662 267
- By fax: 02 9869 0688
- By post: Camp Quality Limited,
  PO Box 400, Epping, NSW 1710

camp quality